Eckhart Cars

PETER JAEGER was born in 1960 in Montreal, Canada. He has worked as a tree planter and library assistant and has taught writing and theory at Dartington College of Arts, the University of Toronto and Royal Holloway, University of London. He currently lives in London, where he teaches at Roehampton University. His previous writing includes *Stretch Conflates* (1997), *Leasing Glass* (1998), *Power Lawn* (1999), *ABC of Reading TRG* (1999) and *Sub-Twang Mustard* (2000).

Also by Peter Jaeger

Stretch Conflates. Buffalo: Tailspin Press, 1997
Leasing Glass. Buffalo: Meow Press, 1998.
Bibliodoppler. London: Writer's Forum, 1999.
ABC of Reading TRG. Vancouver: Talonbooks, 1999.
Power Lawn. Toronto: Coach House Books, 1999.
Sub-Twang Mustard. Calgary: House Press, 2000.
Pollen. Calgary: House Press, 2002.

Eckhart Cars

PETER JAEGER

SALT

PUBLISHED BY SALT PUBLISHING
PO Box 937, Great Wilbraham PDO, Cambridge CB1 5JX United Kingdom
PO Box 202, Applecross, Western Australia 6153

© Peter Jaeger, 2004

The right of Peter Jaeger to be identified as the
author of this work has been asserted by him in accordance
with Section 77 of the Copyright, Designs and Patents Act 1988.

First published 2004

Printed and bound in the United Kingdom by Lightning Source

Typeset in Swift 9.5 / 13

ISBN 1 84471 037 8 paperback

SP

1 3 5 7 9 8 6 4 2

Contents

Acknowledgments

Versions of some of these poems have appeared in *The Capilano Review*, *C.C.C.P.*, *cul-de-qui*, *ecopoetics*, *The Gig*, *The Queen Street Quarterly*, *West Coast Line*, as well as in *Bibliodoppler* (Writer's Forum), *Pollen* and *Sub-Twang Mustard* (House Press), and *The Common Sky: Canadian Poets Against the War* (Three Square Press). Thanks to all the editors for their interest and generous support. Thanks to Rob Holloway of "Up For Air" on Resonance FM in London. Many thanks also to Tim Atkins, derek beaulieu, Charles Bernstein, Andrea Brady, Allen Fisher, Chris Goode, Keith Haartman, Chris and Jen Hamilton-Emery, Robert Hampson, Jeff Hilson and Steve McCaffery. Many thanks to my family for their encouragement, and special thanks to Redell Olsen for bearing gently with my foibles.

Eckhart Cars

It's enough to hand out bread
when you plot a river
for a swimmer in the Yangtse. "I prefer
the airport anyway, I prefer
a person who loves God," he said, but
if you drop away you're lost, and no one
meets you at the airport. Anyone
can place their eyes
against the pieces: "senses
drop away from mind, senses
will obey . . ." There are your knives
and forks, they were the knot
you cut, they can give you
a hundred dollars

or hundreds of dollars. I
blow this horn,
things change. Cranks
of the higher thought
thought about flight.
"Kansas City
has not been hit in the bombing,"
they say, "Keep your eyes
on the freeway, and come over
see us sometime." They strip
the world of things, as the
Live-For-Ever-Man
cottons on: "Yes, we caught them
with an unseen hook."

Faced with a careful selection
of chemical stews, commonly found
plastered to walls or pouring
over heaths, dunes, and stony places,
we should buck up, for perfection
equals normalcy, and we assume
a human power to exceed
the less heroic traits most valued
in our culture — and yet we still encounter
soil, food, and wood as if they launched
a complex illness, showing us a facet
of another truth, which strands us
on upholstery with qualities
of quiet introspection. We

can still believe here, practical
as cars. "It is right
we are true," they say,
and in the speckled fight they seize
a little something—an artificial pond
smeared with nimbus, or a more
common crisis, finicky for instance
at those far high places
where the leaves shine wetly purple
underfoot. All those letters
still caught up—an all expanding
Thing
among the stupid clouds
and papers.

With rain. With sleet, in fact,
which still depends on stuff—
un-nameable, unconcerned with turning
specified, it doesn't speak
except where faith allows (for some)
a cloth to fall away. "I do not know
what nail to bang," they say, "I
do not know
how hard. But still I bang away
at nails and bend them
into shapes unskilled
and bang them so they're banged." Each
fills with news, and the sea returns
to graded universe. Even summer health,

even you—you even count
the future perfect (the hours
will have been evil
and the night—but everyone
believes in speculation. Find yourself
a single pose, a garden's end—
fingers clutching something—what?
Lathered pitch: here
and other places dwelleth
unto versions. How to hope
in exercise, office gossip,
even architecture? I found us
less and less
a cost-efficient question.

Receding yes and less
facted
than a smoking bank. It's
the goods alright, it's
all the same
or half same or shifted same
and ending same: jumbos
keel a blossom
stained by pedals, by
their pads, as roads
and pools and tenants
stuck in traffic lose
the thread
of what you did—

who? Said something—what?
Love and the critical edge
left idle, left
in homilies—lying
with their leaves extinguished
in the rain. Or
in the snow. Doesn't matter
anyway, dust is coming—not
a constable of drumming
but a parachute
unfurling, parking
near the joy, near
the sorrow
happens.

Food for entertaining
wolves and mud—the imbeciles
of myth. Overtones
of sacrificial victims might appear
among the pollinating carpel
or the buckeye ranging
catkins. Their blocks and towers
recommend a person
interfering with your solitary
tune, proven by a day
in the park, which seemed
to offer comfort then. Tired,
us too tired, too many runs
from home on my wheels—

yours—as we lean against
the dash and all the lanes
untangle. The beauty is
we can just go back across the street
and get whatever we want, anytime.
We entertain forgiveness
but prefer another cause—
this is what I think about in meetings,
nodding my head—"I like objects
human-scaled," also
maps—more of us pooling
bashed-out brakes, ribs half-bowed
towards the new frankness,
opening another tin.

Did you learn to capture water on your
fingers (this is what I thought)—I mean, military
water—how it hovers over borders. How to make
our senses mind our minds—the hugeness
of the sky in trains, the town decides
just when to turn—what colour is it?
Sun blush, corn rick, ribbon yellow?
Driving flags to a city
in a city, meetings facing work—
the work of the gift of meeting—
each is real, but shoes get scuffed
on a plinth. They will seem small, like
the boring terror of a dampened habit
speeding through the politics

of city parks, or the fleshy beaks
of borders lending less than single eggs
in recompense for wings, or the same
slamming stones, or the winter-
softened earth. This is our start up,
not that trust appears
and is justified—but understood
against its own background, wanting
hidden pitfalls. What's your premier thinking
at that lurch? When the world—the trees
and lawns and summer clerks—when
all the details leave us stumped, well,
if truth be told, who can cast a pearl,
and who from in this territory stems?

Pollard

not of much
account

a mere hedgerow
by the wayside

blunt lenticels
relished by birds

met by sulphur
wing tips

paper pulp &
broom heads

within its pearly house
silver warting

slender bud burst
bristles

prized as they
kindle well

residing in a quality
of beams

spanning homes, stained
charcoal

bending the oaken
lintel west

a place of singular interest
to myself

that canopy
gathered in bark

for tanning
uphill leather

called forth
as seasons grant

a screen
against dust

a belt
around crops

planting young
blisters, waste

for the risen
alders & their

hacking out
songs –

what we do
with roots

sufficient to afford
every rustic

lathe turning
red & greatly

cherished for
gunstocks

[8]

which led to
willing consent

chipping timber
into flat green cleats

budding
a valued mast

at that delightful spot
an ancient veneer

commanding
the highest eaves

easily struck
from cuttings

above all, the shy
pastoral recess

through which luster
streams

ideal for carving
into plates

Extension of Standard Practice

at least for those who hope
        for overthrow, huge
resources, days after the attack
        easily forgotten, energy
supplies and strategies
        ensuring   uninhibited access
if reactions are
        unpredictable, if used as a base
in an effort to achieve, in
        army manuals, in fact, it
wasn't even reported
        is likely to increase, key
markets, major drug-
        trafficking outlet
major energy reserves
        many people like you
and me, maybe worse
        official doctrine, often on a
shocking scale, should
        the CIA, should
the U.S., soft
        targets, specialist
on the region, strong internal
        radical, that's not the CIA
"uni   lateral   ism", volatile
        is right, Washington
is stepping, Washington
        might determine, we must
remember what is at stake
        what is called low
intensity warfare, with
        ardent wishes, with
credible evidence, with no
        objection, with official
definition, without letup

Pollen

No sooner does an impasse establish itself than plagiarism is likely to set in.

Ambition ruins reading.

As long as we stay with specifics we can only accumulate.

A wandering hand may see itself as playing fair by announcing its target in advance, but a true landscape never emphasises short-term precepts over long-term mull.

All books have their sky.

Most of us can barely even envisage the hints of a plus where warmth once won.

A selection that alleges increase is easier to know than anorexic leisure, for the former insulates the arms of public tags, while the latter merely poses them as lore.

Even when smoothness quivers, there must be something in it that calls out this feeling in us ... which is to say, flat shares affect.

Most prospects are apt to regard secrets as not really touching their own aspiration, but as something exclusive and solitary.

On a slogan a waver perches.

An intentional structure appears most bearable when divided.

Whoever has a gift for compilation ought to be able to learn driftism like any other mechanical art.

Nice people make bad collaborators.

The pantomimes of critical culture no longer exist—but in compensation, all pantomimes now resemble critical culture.

A theory marches on its examples.

The hidden assumption of surrender is that there are claims and there are exits, and that we always remain permissible.

Some select a kinder weight for looking.

Fettered to steer, believing what the lank perceive, the vast majority list at glamour.

And yet we've just begun—true, although the ends are underfoot.

Demand is both valuable and easily understood.

In these circumstances, I would be shirking if I confined myself to a string of reliance; it was my intention to throw light on retrieval.

From our perspective, benefit merely migrates through sanctions.

There are many people who are too tender for theory, and too dignified for poetry—a tangible proof of standards.

The government of homilies is rooted in the family.

We always come back to the question of neo-linearity; if we follow causality, variation remains forcefully removed from engagement.

Many concepts are like the sudden meeting of two workers at the end of a long shift.

The deflection of spectacles modifies struggle.

The gaze is a sort of domination bent from genitives.

One should attempt to classify control only in relation to the consumption of ordinary problems.

Every theory of language that excludes the phrase "cool, daddio" must be incomplete.

The foremost way to read is to skim without considering too much . . . that way tone predominates over incarceration.

When a form doesn't know what to answer, it is usually the result of an accident rather than a conscious action.

Believing in currency and always straining at the virtual; frenetically marginal and proudly dependent; awkward at weather but a genius of tedium; dumb with acumen—can you guess to what type of pornography these traits correspond?

If we distinguish between reverie and dream as two different products, the question of right or wrong remains unanswered.

Undoubtedly, process is no longer merely a twin of verb.

The best way to copy is to re-use referents with pseudo-antediluvian textures.

The only zero co-ordination is that which also co-ordinates the gap that separates it from nothing.

She that finds the split of conversation gains an unspecific consolation.

Brilliant achievement is the achievement of achievement.

Instructions drug us into genre.

Handy is the truce of platitudes.

Unpredictability is not easy, and doubt is hit or miss.

The defenders of constraint will only accept a critique based on statistics.

Does not allegiance feel about the uniqueness of its reverence just as I feel about the uniqueness of mine?

In a crucial sense, function is a testimony to imperatives.

All theory constantly aspires toward the condition of example.

The miraculous regulation, formed of an inconceivable number of independent parts, has evolved to a degree of supply capable of the surplus needed for supposition.

Examples are always more efficacious than we are.

An aporia is a triumph over the self that, like all self mastery, procures new personnel.

Autonomy remains refracted from prevention's news to glaze how precious equals worth.

Aspiration is hard to define—that is part of its mystique—but there is no doubting its ambition.

The doctrine of exits is significant because, among other things, it puts circuits in touch with flight.

[14]

Every narrative can master need, except for the one who has it.

We are close to being nonplussed when we are baffled by bewilderment.

Currency is ripe for lyrical finance.

Read not the form which you can easily tame once it is you.

If there is no speech between vacillation and reliance, no one will dilute haphazard.

The margin looks at its own status, seeing there a guarantee; it acts, and verges not after things extraneous to it.

There is no construction we so much underrate as inaccurate thought, except perhaps erroneous form.

Many are afraid of theory, and more of example.

Every reading meets its Waterloo at last.

We find gloss embodied in economic, military and political inspiration: harnessed to fabrication, its impact effects the quality of struggle and the kinds of route, dodge and stump that govern comment.

At every reading reputation dies.

Many of the chief founders of variety should not be considered genus, but species.

Some remain attached to the logic of clusters, even when historical specificity leads them to believe in surprise.

[15]

Along with the purely life-sustaining function of a yield, a surrender recalls profits which seemingly have no end beyond themselves.

Offering readers too little, and even that, too late.

Many volumes remain affectionate, while some suggest whatever their former tenders may have been.

When two desires meet, their first talk is of design.

Suspension stands out like a beacon of integrity in a sea of the inconsequential.

He reads most who serves best.

The celebration of resolution during elections has been highly advantageous to notation.

I dreamed that, as I wandered by an image, bare conjecture suddenly was practice.

Contemporary proportion is rooted in the awareness of how self-centred guidelines can no longer be adequately understood only as psychological or physiological drives manifesting themselves in social directions.

Props usurp supports.

An illustration is an honest form sent to live abroad for its presumptions.

Here they shoot a form first and read it afterwards.

The freedom of codes is a relative freedom from the pressure of appraisal, from the craving for improv, from identification with semblance, and from the correspondence originating in such attachments.

To embrace constraint does not mean to indulge in it.

When I read, who knows whether relationship is not amusing itself with me more than I with it.

Nearly four in every ten alive were once a party due to borrow.

Homage is the realization of all that is practically expedient.

Prototypes afraid of love love their fear.

A little of everything and nothing thoroughly, after the skirmish method.

It is private reading that offends; to read in the open is no scandal at all.

The true rime is the slaying of distance and the answer to all conditions needed for manufacture.

It is a stupidity next to none, to busy oneself with the correction of contour.

To lower the cost of incongruity, customers need more patient, committed evaluations and less of a hunger for dividends.

Disparity is easy to cure; resemblance, impossible.

Caesura is to amber light as verdant is to rococo.

Approval favours context.

If we had no books we would not take so much pleasure in noticing them in others.

Legislators are the unacknowledged poets of the world.

If one judges cultural critique by its effect, it is more like poetry than medicine.

It is less fun to distrust one's books than to be deceived by them.

Assessment is always fooled by desire.

The reputation of a form is often gained in much the same way as money; if you insist on the quiet exchange of a confidential agreement, the rest will follow by itself.

Feeble under gentle would have brutalised our asking price.

One improves a guarantee with material wealth, while another improves an impulse by looking straight at sever, and then oscillating on results.

It takes great imaginative skill to conceal one's Imaginary.

A figure is an aim that contains a systems of aims.

We are at an apex of conventions.

We only read our little standards to persuade ourselves we have no large ones.

Nothing prevents us from being conjectural so much as the desire to appear so.

I wish to preach not the doctrine of the ignoble concept, but of the strenuous shape.

Choose a theory as you choose a friend.

The great brink takes root in clarifying the way that uncertainty increases; it is brimmed with affection for the loose end.

Surplus clerks a mathematic escapade.

Show me a syllabus and I'll show you a parapraxis.

Personification is the beginning and end of legalism.

The volatility of originality makes timing the essence of success; those who time their innovations correctly earn fortunes, while those who do not are worth less than their bibliography.

The purest readers are those who love legislation the most.

Inclinations to dodge are more praiseworthy than inclinations to hedge.

Every apex sections.

Interpretations are given to contradict whereabouts.
Every time I read a book I lose a reason.

The collage is to the lyric as the international bank deposit is to the currency of its origin.

Circulation usually wins the battle, while paraphrase gets the credit.

Paradise is not having to respond.

Distribution is the best of all devices for leading questions by the nose.

It is my ambition to say in ten philosophies what others say in a single example.

Assumptions in my heart I bore, long after they were heard no more.

Success has always been a great doctrine.

The impulse toward volume is the impulse toward property, but more stimulating is the composition which excites consequence; where assets and outcome are, impetus amasses.

Effect is invisible to the reader who has none.

Diagrams lubricate theory.

Examples are nothing else but the intermission of critical prose.

The more I read, the more I lie.

Every function has a volume ... if only the reverse were also true.

Take a form and throw it up in the air—you will see by that way where theory blows.

If the consummate form of result is narrative, each break must have a corollary—it must be a self-evident alibi, enveloping a flash of parallels.

Let them read so long as they fear.

Lyrics are the wine of poetry ... when stained, a little cold water does the trick, as long as one gets to the material in time.

It is not only fine abstractions that make fine facts.

For some, offence is a satisfying collection of contemporary moods.

A standstill is a criticism of life under the conditions fixed for it by conjecture.

Not deep, the concept sees, but wide.

So various are the gadgets of taste.

Every gentle demo bolsters.

Shirkers of the world unite.

Midwest

credit's gloat, never
dearth—do the seared
gain of sifting you
lurch on tick, lending

a stoop for hire, lesser
than teasing crime: hi-fi
moods a tune's insolvent
night: the skiff of

flailing loud
and saturation,
slack, flinted
floods the yucky good

if fluted woods
recast a spin, content
to poke no sight
and rag absorbing binding

strings of animal families
are at last. Slaking a penny
on my banking, as the
clanly faces seed

asleep—I grow
a back-up blameless: I
bark, the place a
beached-out driver

further rates. Case on, biz
blight, chastened
row of freight? Flaunting
bummer fair, Pacific

list—misers as is un,
by maples, horses
cast a mix until
they catalogue

rest, masked—could
they bow, count
as hurdles, cross your heart
and hope to die

on bold reductions, legends
debit—run up a hill, grazing
receptive as whims—
did they minus your

display: relentless bruise
if driving ever
fans a book
on the Tupperware fades

fax of landed hung with
flake, who
in cancellation, they
from whims

here is now again, as
marts haul
food, how they shine and
how could they not?

husk of wolf at the door—
I hate them and lie
in lifted deuce, renting
the learn, with its

lore of roiling flophouse
shredder lease. Let us
butter fingers, length
of their parting—

taxes prompt fallow
a happiness
manufactured: will we still
hate them?

purely nab to gain
mended for flicker
or mess from another—how
of gun. Ten-four

lending, bland
mark on lessons
fluster, you
on price. Highway

or will we still lie?
You may surely stay
pacing a river, the
all per day. Sun elides

pertains to wheat, where
place—bought
places—craving just
a prayer in malls

they need not
pure a call for strife—I
was basking O say
in the learning

receiving a middle
lecture not for long
said. Their rooms do not
see that marching

so guiltless
bores a sheen
shrunk to think the payments
smack of less resign—

steel, the seared
face who bask in names
as if stone on the
corny screen

double-bubble
rain or gliding
three if by news
then vote, and lead us

to a blinding perforation,
cowboy truck, breaded
weather and un-
furling flag

on rigs, how their
victory can yodel
troops, whips
where you know land

cheers us up
and sends us into
all the highest, leave
the rest

So They Say

If you like, you can examine the figures
as you track along my shelter, still devoted
to drinking tea and other pleasant pastimes
whose amplitude alone determines energy.

I stick to this, though fountains lull me
into privacy. There we stand in postures
to this day, a goodness held ten times the size of ours,
thinkable, self-poised—a rugged worth half-seen,

new fluffed in truth with triumphs choosing
all the likely crowds of value. Not here
the learning wade, not yet. For who is not summer?
Already ripening, nearly done, scarce

will find his own, so that many wait for stuff. We detect
quivering with measuring as filament turns serious:
rise stones the hardy system, which their hands
hold slightly utmost, a pointer weighing nothing.

Above that friendly or nostalgic street the virtual dimensions of the earth showed us a fear of solids, or so it seemed. Nothing happened to us, and we didn't want it to, for we bore within us fantasies. And so we looked upon the moon's first quarter, thinking how it shook our youngest to an urge.

Each day my way to the studio took me through the gardens by the progeny of dung beetles and sacred scarabs. We spent a few days below the summit, clarifying the secret dreams of animals who trek an atmospheric zone across their own ambition. The function of their photographs enlarged the scale of those who live among

an oblique rhythm. That was their general approach, concentrated, but because there were generally very few stars in the vicinity, I felt no more important than a camera. The result

was a vagueness beyond credit, performing in ever widening circles, until it touched the next in line. But anyway, those customs were for more advanced students, not the actual beginners, busy as they were with the killing of golden-crested wrens.

How I missed the badge you kept in secret
till you stilled what more increased its want.

We walked parched fields and the threads
of an antique four-line clef, indifferent to the tongs

of therapy, for what we knew to be good and pleasing
went away, and we wandered; we were all in every way

instructed by the blazing tang of horseradish
chewed without respite for years under ornamental maples

while the shade of the earth, so vastly esteemed
scattered in fields like another hope's amenity.

The more awkward they were, the more instructive an example they offered us. We had no packs to carry and it seemed delightful to walk through a dusky forest with all these books, my nose still running at the smell of your general principles. We got so

into moving pictures, five-part time with varied slumbers seemed less and less like hummingbirds flitting among tropical flowers. At first they were party to an overwhelming tumult, culminating later that night in a tendency to become more and more compact

and uniform in mass, like some kind of moneyed trance on the boil in Bern, Switzerland, or along the original way into a city. There we also dwelt within the matted undergrowth of everyday decisions, homesick, lulled by fictional butterflies who complained and had headaches

and were pale. We shed nocturnal shadows, so happy because there at least our wants were heated and our socks could dry on the yonderly plants. Yes, I should have felt content, I know, and should have slept the fancy I required, and yet, as I thought it over, the phonograph grinded on tirelessly,

locking me into a singular vision. At that stage, also, we decided to bolster up the strength of elementary examples. They lighted us with ambitions, and in their luminosity, everyone saw an important relation.

A Book I Am Dreaming

A broadcast
for strands?

You resume
but still effect

the author of a dream, awake
to basic pretence—

dwindle trigger, long
for love, resort

to earning but
chloroform a butterfly

dreaming of a human, dreaming
carved from knack. I

chuck dun, scrimp
afresh as cities kindle

up in clumps, contour
in-laws nap

when dope delays
veneer & misty

furniture. Dream Line Lie
Detection, dream on,

on to the heart of the sunrise—
mumble now enfolds

a curl, my cheapest
function, limp

thread—as if
these gravities delete

the fun of yearning. I
relish dirt, hushed

by anti-candy. Neanderthal
eccentrics

& their nick-nacks
run dumbfounded, lulled

by the dreaming world— a kernel
of a nocturne

or a threat
the public found

in next of kin. We is
glow directed, gloating

over piltdown
weirdos. If you add

to adoration, you
solicit nurdsville—

well-behaved it shares my
green support. I yield

for goofs— I
catalogue

a squad of Dream Home
Fashions; acquisition

infiltrates whenever good
identifies with gang

Sub-Twang Mustard

troglo
>blip whiff
>sole re-
>strudled scut

bump
>ditch or
>hocus
>
>dashing my some
>simple, it is
>
>a sometimes
>plus of
>
>it or
>ditch, or
>
>sometimes
>just paired

fur
>wig t'pink
>astanga candy

zafu
>clod
>drizzl
>putt

mown
> sought out
> numb & its
> crush, jaw
> dodgy anyhow
> unsorted though
> fed up
> sack

tain
> in the tip
> went at
>
> cover, loan is
> friend to a
>
> was, no
> but

won't
> range, won't
> settle kiddo

polite
> cathole yoghurt
> yoghurt butter
> butter zoo

cleanhead

    shimmerdent, tag—
    soon the slutch
    cactus

zip

    inside
    job but for
    peck
    batter
    plonk &
    angle etc.

haiku

    benches

    tinkle

    gum

    thorn

light

    when even
    chuffs, holding
    carny sash &
    full but
    not that little
    prairie

[38]

sushi

      so filly
      subtle &

      it abandons
      them, who

      slum
      fantabulous

trotter

      bamboo
      comma
      dracula

zone

      were my
      plasterd

      iffy to

      might be

      were

bond

      world who
      tinkle
      dot sops

[39]

damp
　　　　why would any
　　　　lope

crupper
　　　　what
　　　　is it, as if

　　　　grommet had
　　　　milksop

　　　　to fashion, its
　　　　manifold skids a

　　　　whack or some
　　　　veggie fumble

volume
　　　　sub-twang mustard

paw
　　　　out
　　　　at elbows, as the

　　　　crow flies
　　　　pin

item
> nah put on
> nah o.k., to

> job some
> kick, a

> jack and
> colder jolt

slick
> I'm afraid you
> can't
> mutt

rent
> so spindle, so
> modish scrunch

quench
> herd, uh huh
> jerky ampersand

talc

        leech to my
        park or
        ankh dims
        plash

tamp

        & family the
        math of
        afterall
        grade, what
        grade of the
        blanket this
        gorge might
        collect, we
        or even
        lovely tethers

cinch

        ok love, you
        subtle
        phlox

Narrow

Those who steer across or drive over spend every. Even while I was
getting and applying, I was already full. Finally I sold. Upon the
threshold, however, I hung the starting that I took. There was
lingering and still, though gradually away. I walked all through
for I knew sleep would only accumulate. When I reached towards,
I barely consisted of against equipment. I wanted to, but there
were, and I could not. On the first I climbed what used to be built
and must have had, though most of all now prevails embracing.
More would violate. I watched rather carefully but found almost
stubbornly utterly, as if merciful had taken help. Indeed, such
must, for it verges. It was in spite so I took after very and put on
itinerant even.

At last I was impressed by a huge of several in a craggy wide, but
before I stretched it fell. As I was plodding through, I tarried on
whose rest is said to call. He was wooden amid before and talked
so tall I ranged. A narrow trailed between banks of dripping,
leading us across. I was surely situated for I had an opportunity
and thought its name was somewhat, but by and by I came to
small in a dark near hot, completely wrapped. There was such a
hardly. The first was able to gain a certain no longer to pestering,
and it was with mild that I thought about the plea who had
passed burning. His gate was counted among and many had, each
leaving his own. I myself walked between laden with thick and
the tints before

a sure soft
section surely

stood in this
sure soft give,

gave and is
sure

[43]

Pushing towards I crossed and walked between divided. It had, however, and nothing but grey scattered. It was the season of a certain, so I went to look, asking every on the way, but no one had, and the sun went even. I cut across, saw dazed, and put up. On the following I found the middle altogether crossing when I came to the ruined, about a mile and a half towards. I could not refrain for there was lonely and bitter in front remembering frail. It was filthy with rough spread out on a dim between leaking and the raids. I trod because. Passing through arrived, I asked, and was told that I must. The direction was still there by the side, buried in deep. I wanted of course but the muddy after early and my own stopped just with its trance shaped exactly.

When I lay in the roaring, clear spanned, so I tried to fall suppressing but was simply. This better known enlarged into a spacious and there were hundreds where countless thronged. I was pleased though it was mere. Strangely enough, however, no one offered. After much I found a miserable, and spending uneasy, wandered where long came to an end. It is here that away passed empty. The main greeted my utterly, and as I climbed one of the called, I saw running pour into big. Ruined was located, thus blocking and forming against. These buildings, too, would have, but thanks to a covering they were at least. Next I looked at puny and arrived at blocked. The gate-keepers were extremely, for very few dared this difficult under.

At a goal there was terribly uncertain, so I found who walked with a curved and a firmly. I myself followed afraid of might. The mountains were so thickly hushed through stumbling or at last shedding. I was indeed, for accidents had always. So I visited a rich and deep of wandering. Finding at last, I spent. I left soon, however, for I wanted to see the full with the tucked in somewhat. The sky was unusually. After a pleasant I went to honour the hushed who shone brilliantly upon white, so that ground seemed first, though ever since a handful rained on fancies. The change-able prevented full, again to the pink so I sailed off aided by else and dotted with mingled.

Early Gardening

a ransom of 3 million crowns
to build signs of breath or
shadows wandered wild

about 1 foot square, now
obtaining loud
along the streets and walk's

accumulation—came
to my knees with silent
winter crops to grow,

banks I wandered, reading
an amalgam of gold
and silver—alert

among the pomegranate here
depicted, short
our limestone

clung, they demand
the predator behind each
creature—great

at the fall of night
a serpent lurks
beheaded—no

description of
botanical scholarship,
astronomy

of morn, if we wander
not too far away, we're
given to by gladiators,

[46]

orders of the city prefect—
spectators infuriated
by two springs—laurel

of antiquity, cedar,
cypress and poplar,
in the swamps, city

and orchard enclosures laid out
pools and smaller paths, cosmetics
and perfumes, solace of our

cowrie shells, metal coins—
doll-house size, sculpted
crocus lily and

water-loving
data recedes lore, for its
keen breath from laws

and legal records gain
discovery, serious even
as we write off how it fled—

fashioned from electrum, a natural
day in silence did we drift, ideas
spread the first merchant

banker
gotten alter decoration,
invented for minting coins—

admitted this was so and
peopled this terrific trance
from a grander perception

of landscape, intruders
and a formal pool—goutweed
for salads, evening airs

wander grottoes and mossy
nymphaeums,
hunting parks on the banks

of the river, I wandered
in a forest thoughtlessly,
impression in your mouth—

smell is there—the cool
north, forests of scrub oak
rightful cause gives breath, served

in the lore and forest glades, in flooding
choice of sites, a copper shortage
which the very scent

defends—the world in wood
is painted green, drifted
on some legacy

persisting till they suffix
just your tilt, throughout
those overshadowed

avenues affording leather
money: pieces of
white deer skin,

legal angels, lonely stream—
high walls protect
the garden lotus

[48]

and the marshy gold
papyrus—stretch in the shade
of my sycamore, walk

on the banks of my water,
letters more than a thousand years
before paintings, new layouts

presiding over ferns, nothing
grew except a giant reed—
coins of lily

already arrived when last
the pleasure gardens—our small
knowledge of silver

6 miles in circumference,
temples, houses, garden plans, species of trees—
almanacs in a concourse

on a vast scale, if we lose
sight of one wave, flowers
mainly valued, run

into arenas
or receding pools—annual
flood plains and species of box

ornamental plants, lips
and breath approve our steps—
only two gardens appear

out in early morn, in the morning
light—denarii now pennies
with a p and not a d—

opium poppies
flourish in moist mud, solid
shade's essential feature

red recedes, employing
nursery gardeners
relating to useful plants—

remaining statues
rifled, ornament
machines of good green fortune

issued us in
Samarkand
a traveller approaching

helps preserve the buried traces
paying "through the nose" i.e.
slits the nose of those remiss

in paying debts, something
like the oldest garden
room—sweet thoughts

do even now refresh our labours,
token skulls and feathers
close the credit

grows a plot in his
monastery—the printing press
soon modified

for minting coins, vineyards
all surround through trade and
conquest, separate

combatants killed to furnish flowers
for medicine, cooking
was of course the aromatic bay

a watered grove with trim
shade, questing
taproots, irrigation boosts and

plus produces
less, pollinating
winds and avenues

Martyrologies

He admitted that this was so, and after a short imprisonment he was beheaded. He was broken limb by limb. She was burned to death on an islet in the river. Whereupon they were buried alive. But eventually she died from her sufferings. For this insubordination they were twice decimated. She was executed by being stabbed in the throat (a common Roman form of execution). He was himself arrested and put to death amongst supernatural happenings. In a drunken fury they set on him, pelting him with bones, and although one of them tried to save him, he was killed by a blow on the head with an axe. After doing all he could to safeguard his flock, he submitted to death. They shot him down and flung his body into his burning church. They were arrested as apostles and beheaded. She refused to renounce her faith, whereupon her father was ordered himself to put her to death. At length she was tied in a net and thrown to a bull, which gored her to death. When they broke in on him he was sitting quietly at a desk reading. He encountered fierce opposition and was soon put to death with eighteen companions. Within a short time of one another these young men were murdered, each of them refusing to allow his men to defend him. They were therefore burnt alive. Urged not to make her children motherless by her obstinacy, she replied, "God will look after them," and went to the stake. She was brought before the prefect, and upon her refusing an act of idolatry she was sentenced to be stifled to death in the bathroom of her own home. He struck her three ineffective blows, and she was left to linger three days before she died. They were martyred by being burned alive in a sandpit. While Christians were praying at their tomb, the emperor ordered its entrance to be blocked up and the worshippers were left there to perish. She was beheaded and her body thrown into the river. He may have succumbed to hardships in exile, but later statements that he was beheaded are not supported by any historical evidence. The proceedings were read over, and she was sentenced to death by the sword. He gave a generous gift to the executioner, blindfolded himself, and his head was struck off. The man in a rage threw him down the steps of the tribune, killing him outright. So far from being distressed, she rejoiced at her son being a Martyr, and went cheerfully to torture and death. He was fabled to have carried his severed head to the place of his burial. Her father found her there and when she refused to return home with him, slew her and the priest. He was tied to a tree and shot with arrows till his body was "like a thistle covered with prickles"; then his head was struck off. The governor ordered him to be tortured to exhort more precise information, but they remained mute and were beheaded. A later legend said that he was put to death by having his intestines wound out of his body on a windlass. Having protested against the idolatrous festival, he was stoned to death by the people. She put on a male dress and became abbot of a monastery; she was accused of misconduct and cleared herself by declaiming her sex; she then went to Rome, and, after various fabulous occurrences, was beheaded for her faith. He tried to induce her to show honour to the gods, and on her refusal she was tortured and burnt to death; a white dove flew out of her mouth and a fall of snow covered her dead body. Her acts consist chiefly of a catalogue of the tortures which she miraculously survived, until she was thrown to wild beasts. He was roasted to death together with his wife and two sons. They were brought before four different judges and sentenced to die in differing ways, the mother last of all. He shut them in a cell, threatening to sell them into prostitution if they would not apostatize; they remained firm and were beheaded. They were drowned in a well. It was ordered that they should be stripped naked, herded onto a frozen pond, and kept there; to help break down their resistance a fire was kindled and warm baths were prepared where they could see them, but by the next day most of them were dead. They were shut up in leaden boxes and thrown into the river. As the flames enveloped them, they stretched out their arms in token of the Lord's victory praying to him till they gave up their souls. He survived torment for a whole night, and was killed by a blow on the head from an axe. His body was hurled from a height into the river. He was murdered by sea rovers. They were eventually martyred, their hearts fearing lest their old religion and customs should be changed. He was very bald, and when he was given a chance to sacrifice he replied: "no, not until hair again grows from my head," whereat the emperor held him up to ridicule by having a goat's skin tied over his head before crucifying him with five others. The fair one was killed outright, but the dark one was first put to slow torture; their bodies were thrown into the river and heavenly portents followed. An attempt was made to break her on a spiked wheel, but it fell to pieces and she was unhurt, while some of the spectators were killed by flying splinters; finally she was beheaded. He was either starved to death, or, more probably, killed by the sword. He was betrayed, condemned, and crucified. He was stoned to death. He was killed by the sword. They were sewn up in skins of wild beasts, and then worried by dogs until they expired. They were dressed in shirts stiff with wax, fixed to axle-trees, and set on fire. After refusing to sacrifice to Neptune, he was cast first into a hot lime kiln, and, being drawn from thence, was thrown into a scalding bath, where he expired. After being scourged, he was compelled to hold fire in his hands, while papers dipped in oil were put to his sides and lighted; his flesh was then torn with hot pincers, and at last he was dispatched by wild beasts. They were obliged to pass, with their already wounded feet, over thorns, nails, sharp shells, etc., others were scourged till their sinews and veins lay bare, and, after suffering the most excruciating tortures, were destroyed by the most terrible deaths. He was carried before the pro-consul, condemned, and put to death in the market place. They were condemned to be first scourged and then beheaded. For refusing to worship Commodus as Hercules, they were likewise put to death. After remaining in prison for a considerable time, he was beat to death with a club. She was first torn by wild beasts, and then killed by the sword. He was severely scourged and then hanged up by the feet, and boiling water was poured over him; he was afterwards worried by wild beasts and at last beheaded. When he refused to wear a laurel crown bestowed by the emperor, and called himself a Christian, he was scourged and put to death. He was banished and destroyed. He gave so much offence to the government by collecting the acts of the martyrs that he suffered martyrdom, after having held his dignity only forty days. Forty two were all beheaded in one day, and their heads fixed on the city gates. He was tied to a wild horse and was dragged through fields, stony places, and brambles, till he died. They were slain without trial and buried in heaps; sometimes fifty or sixty being cast into a pit together. He was seized and suffered martyrdom by decapitation. He was frequently tortured, but remained inflexible; and, though often brought from prison for execution, was again remanded, to suffer greater cruelties; he was at last put into a leathern bag with a number of serpents and scorpions and thrown into the sea. He was broken on a wheel, but his torments only inspired him with fresh courage, and he even smiled at his persecutors; he was at length beheaded. The mouth of a cavern was closed up with them inside, and they were starved or smothered to death. He was fastened by the feet to the tail of a bull; the enraged animal was driven down the steps of the temple, by which the martyrs brains were dashed out. He was beaten with iron rods, set upon a wooden horse, and had his limbs dislocated; he endured these tortures with such fortitude and perseverance, that he was ordered to be fastened to a large gridiron, with a slow fire under it, that his death might be more tedious. All 300 of them were suffocated in a burning lime-kiln. He was condemned to walk on burning coals, and is said to have walked over them without damage before being beheaded. 6,666 of them were put to death. He was seized, tortured, and then burnt alive. They had stones fastened about their necks and were driven into the sea. They were first chained to a post, then a gentle fire put to the soles of their feet, which contracted the callus till it fell off from the bone; then flambeaux just extinguished were put to all parts of their bodies, so that they might be tortured all over, and care was taken to keep them alive by throwing cold water on their faces, and giving them some to wash their mouths, lest their throats should be dried up with thirst and choke them; thus their miseries were lengthened out, till at last, their skins being consumed, and they just ready to expire, they were thrown into great fire and their bodies burned to ashes, after which their ashes were thrown into some river. His body was torn every day in seven different parts till the skin and flesh were entirely mangled and he expired. They were ordered to embark on a ship which was set on fire, and they all perished in flames. His skull was fractured by a tile thrown at him from the roof of a house. They were delivered over to the secular power and burnt. They were driven in to the Alps, where great numbers were frozen to death. 3000 were suffocated by having fagots placed in their mouths and set on fire. All the men were cut to pieces; all the women and children were driven into a large barn, which was set on fire, and everyone perished in the flames. Nothing was to be heard but the groans of men who lay weltering in their blood; the lamentations of mothers, who, after being cruelly ill treated by the soldiery, had their children taken from them and dashed to pieces before their eyes. Numbers were hanged, drowned, tied to trees and pierced with prongs, thrown from precipices, burnt, stabbed, racked to death, worried by dogs, and crucified with their heads downwards. Sixty thousand persons of different ages and both sexes were murdered. 180 persons were committed to the flames. 5000 men, women and children were put to the sword. 20 were roasted on spits. The greatest slaughter was in the first three days, in which were said to be murdered above 10,000 men and women, old and young, of all sorts of conditions. Her constancy brought about the conversion of 500 soldiers, who were straightaway beheaded with her. Within the space of one month 30,000 were slain. There died in this massacre, within a few days, fifty or threescore persons. Fifty-seven were butchered in one day. Great numbers suffered in confinement till they perished. He was set upon an ass with his face to the tail, which he was obliged to hold in his hand; in this condition he was led to the marketplace, amidst the acclamations of the populace; after which he was mutilated and burnt, till at last he died with pain. She was seized and carried through the streets with a paper mitre on her head; after mocking and beating her, the multitude fell upon and destroyed her. He was led to the place of execution in a garment painted with demon figures, and had a paper mitre put on his head by way of derision; having been placed on a pile of fagots, the fire quickly reached him. She was racked with such severity that she expired a week later of the wounds and bruises. The veins in his arms and legs were opened and he gradually sank to death without apparent pain. He was cast out the window into the street, where his head was struck off: the people then cut off his arms and drew his mangled body three days through the streets, after which they took it to the place of execution and there hanged it by its heels, to the scorn of the populace. Some had their heads cleft in twain, their arms and hands cut off. They were conveyed to three deep mines near the town, and were thrown into each where they perished miserably. Their hands and feet were tied behind them, and they were thrown into the river. He was killed as he lay sick in bed. he and his wife were tied back to back and burnt. He was hung on a crossbeam with a fire underneath and broiled to death. He was hacked into small pieces. His mouth was filled with gunpowder and head blown to atoms. They derided and mocked him; hunted him like a wild beast till ready to expire with fatigue; made him run the gauntlet, each striking him with their fists or with ropes; scourged him with wires; tied him up by the heels till the blood started out of his nose and mouth; hung him up by the arms till they were dislocated, and then had them set again; burning papers, dipped in oil, were placed to his feet; his flesh was torn with red hot pincers; he was put to the rack and most cruelly mangled; boiling lead was poured upon his feet; and, lastly, a knotted cord was twisted about his forehead in such a manner as to force out his eyes until he died. They stripped him naked and covered him alternately with ice and burning coals until he expired beneath the torment. At length his voice was interrupted by the flames, which soon put an end to his mortal life. When the flames began to envelop him he sang another hymn. She was executed by being strangled before the faggots were kindled. He was tied up in a sack, thrown into the river, and drowned. He

[57]

was burnt in the market of a village. He was first beheaded, and afterwards burnt to ashes. The executioner offered to strangle him before the fire was lighted, but he would not consent, telling him that he defied the flames; and, indeed, he died with such composure amidst them, that he hardly seemed sensible of pain. Many were doomed to perpetual imprisonment, others to perpetual banishment; but the greater number were put to death either by hanging, or drowning, or burning, the rack, or burying alive. An order was given to drown him in prison, and the executioner accordingly forced him into a large tub; but because he struggled and got his head above water, the executioner stabbed him in several places with a dagger until he expired. Some were suspended from trees, their bodies left to be devoured by beasts or birds of prey. He was co cruelly used that his body burst, and he expired in the greatest agonies. They were stripped naked and whipped to death with iron rods. They were hewn into pieces with swords. They were thrown from a high tower. He had his ear bitten off, was stabbed, and thrown into a ditch. He had an iron chain, to which a great stone was suspended, fastened to his body; he was then laid on a plank, with his face upwards, and rowed between two boats out to sea; the boats then separated, and, by the weight of the stone, he was sunk. He was led through the streets, wearing only the image of the devil upon his head and his breeches painted with flames; his right hand was cut off and fixed on a pole and his flesh was scorched with flaming torches before he was burnt to ashes at the stake. He was bound and thrown down a precipice; in the fall a branch of a tree caught hold of the ropes that fastened him, and suspended him midway, so that he languished for several days till he perished of hunger. She had her limbs separated from each other; the parts were then hung on a hedge. Several men, women, and children were flung from the rocks and dashed to pieces. She was thrown down one of the precipices. She had her flesh mangled till she expired. She was cut to pieces in a cave. She had one end of a stake thrust into her body, and the other end being fixed in the ground, she was left to perish.

His four children were killed before his eyes. He was fastened to the tail of a mule, dragged through the streets amidst the accusations of a mob who stoned him; they took him to the river side, struck off his head, and left it with his body unburied on the bank. At ten years of age she was roasted alive. They were hung up by hooks affixed to their bodies, and left to expire. He had his features mangled, and was other wise injured by sharp weapons, till he bled to death. They had their mouths stuffed with gunpowder and their heads blown to atoms. He had the nails of his toes and fingers torn off with hot pincers and holes bored through his hands with the point of a dagger; he next had a cord tied around his middle and was led through the streets with a soldier on each side of him; at every turning the soldier on his right hand side cut a gash in his flesh and the soldier on his left hand side struck him with a bludgeon; at length he was led to a bridge where his head was cut off and thrown with his body into the river. He had his eyes put out, was flayed alive, and divided into four parts, which were placed on the four principle houses of the city. They were driven into the river and stoned to death. He was shot in the neck, mutilated, stabbed, and his carcass was given to the dogs. She was cut to atoms. They deprived him of one limb after another so gradually as to cause him the utmost agony; finding that he bore his sufferings with unconquerable fortitude, they stabbed him to the heart, and gave his body to be devoured by dogs. He was seized with some books and was burned. After his legs were burned up to the stumps, and but a small fire was left under him, two of the inhuman monsters who stood on each side of him pierced him with their halberds, and lifted him up as far as the chain would reach, while he, raising his half-consumed hands, cried unto the people these words: "None but Christ, none but Christ!" and so, being let down again from their halberds, fell into the fire, and there ended his life. They took each other by the hand, and after embracing, submitted themselves to the tormentors, who, fastening them to the stake, soon lighted the faggots, and terminated their mortal life and care. His sufferings were dreadful, for the wood was green, and would not burn, so that he was choked with smoke ; and moreover, being set in a pitch barrel with some pitch still by the sides, he was therewith sore pained, till he got his feet out of the barrel; at length one standing by took a fagot stick, and striking at the ring of iron about his neck and then upon his head, he shrank down on one side of the fire, and was so destroyed. He was struck on the head so violently that his brains fell out, and his dead corpse fell down into the fire. He was struck with a staff so that he fell amid the flames and expired, or rather rose to heaven to live for ever.

Buoyant

ballast spreads

in tunes / waves

in the drink   takes

a bath   birth

twists

the water breaks—

broke

we shop for buckets

soaked

to the skin churning

silt   an ocean

clear as quiet

tubs   spouts

a little streamlet

over brine &

scratches

housing into grains

pours

or drizzles: "very hard work but it's good to dig"

high tide

clunking

flotsam

resting loosely

in the current   a

community tap-stand

first pulled

to drink   then

a cloud thrown out

beyond

the river's bend

and in the midst of all

a cleaner pool   flexing

effortless

as flippers   wet

as a rag   in goggles

plugged

full to bursting a

   duct   got

         yourself

    into hot water

      jug

stopped up with mud

        & oaken spiles

   keeps

    the oldest sap

      inside what town

 by river or

       by sea shore what

    labour looks

       to drowning

   as we gulp reposing distillation

walking miles

       fetch a pail

  we'll never

                    swim   leaving

                              the famous bottle

                                        in that "wilderness

        of sorts," measured out

                          in leagues or fathoms

                all the rest

                          plunges at

                    a quality of life

                                        through cleaner pumps

        pots of rain

                                        no longer do the trick—

                          drop me

                in the flood   all

                    the headlong torrents

                                        troubled waters

        tanks & tins crammed

                          by creatures   stroke

                              of the fluke

[64]

snared

             into fog   illness

       caused by unsafe

spills   raining cats &

          roped with pounds

       some with moats

           while pools

hurl up kelp

                green quiet

in their veins

        & marrow splashing

         at their luck   lost

    in foam

      a stranger

          in the downpour

      puts all hope

on bathing

      coral wall

                                          blue shading

      several billion more

                        who never float   never

                             find a trough   labour

  still unfinished

                sculling

                           near a black-eyed

    swan   upon

          the widening stream

    clean as a whistle

                            under moss

      the gully funnels &

                  we bail out

      waterproof

Sitting

A commune who we know by rote, a
flag is not an exercise in bread. Alabaster

of a mind in pain—this is what I think about,
acoustic woods, I now say what I think.

Again and again how zero—how often of
censure be the wits kept free, and

altering her mind amid the loud distractions
of a felted brain—such splendour

and what it does. Whatever breaks the bonds
of interstice and not for safety only—

at the nose cone, deciduous stone. A dim
attention I may win, pressed by thoughts

attentive hills. Ere we are aware of
oat-brown bread that sent us

lies, like a wheel of warmth
because they come from depth. Pleased

before my view intrudes at times
along the coast of a flattening wave,

breaks. Attending the viewless
intellect, careless stillness of a

cheerfulness in industry of body and of
meditative peace, I like

counting but feeling the rise and fall, then
dance attendance at your heels

in demurest meditation—I still can't get
distracted in a stir, deceived by muscles

as you doze, brain bewildered little stone. My mind
during those sittings—aware of whence

an ear, with head intent, without gripping, as
every one attends. Fair dreams before

eyes, distracted and amazed, discovered—
overawed, attentive

failure when thinking of my own beloved
grains, but doubt is passing—

focus there, as if to tell yourself how quiet
folded hands, today, seem important. From

friends, whose brains are more than their own
mindfulness of sky—till meaning on vacancy

says goodbye to fading who remains. Their subtle
hands, where gentle springs to witness

how easy we get lost, how it dissolves. If
you've done everything to secure

impatience—not merely qualities of sitting, but
prone in a boyish tunnel of snow, or living through

a river of cold dirt. Attention now
held in a secure garage. May you never

find in yourself that meeting, breaking. Calm
is racked with doubt, not esteemed yet always

knows, resting like pyramids or
thunderstones—said to have fallen, to

lose your mind on mountains black and bare, but
contemplating your appointed task, so that

you remain. Take the common
part from knitted brow, between

belief and moral frame may hover till
your patient thought—the hue of

mind—well, into that cell, our
forms proceed—boredom, for example, or

mysticism charged with faith. It
prompts a passion for pearls, as if

cause and effect were not a question—his
own assumptions he did there endure. I

mull over an early evening in the falling
of our 'whens' and 'hows'—can these

hold our fate with gentleness, thinking
of stones? They will be raised to the rank of

the world, an ampler mind's attention
held on desert sand, or hearing sounds dimly thud

on the earth with laboured thought. Lock it up
with peace and broken shoulders,

purpose built for brimming. Now
a recompense for grey, refreshing ease—

simply felt and purely touched so far
releasing always warmer when attention

leaves out epaulettes—we began
distracted by borders—sprawl

and span for such a distance. Think then of
spaces—counting after, counting before, not

the mind's eye as it flits—fatigue
to the point where fear makes us quote, but

the favourites in thunder, no
thinking what it teaches us

in the caves of our collectives, wherever
we can recognise clouds. Do thoughts

unite in kindred quietness? Throngs
through my mind like drowsy tinklings,

towards a kind of church, aware of the dark and
difficult blindness. But I can feed

on older parts of distance: the result
runs at limits always tinged

with dimness beyond credit, where
conquest isn't real until the ritual of taking

which prevents. First dawn and thought
flown provokes an ample

flash. Vague thoughts are these, vested
winds from where attention springs. Bear it

with my nostrils at the peak, shins flat
on what it is I take

Bibliodoppler

Reverse the stock in trade
to script a ransom. Forget
to mirror astrolabe
whenever rental enters
temple's check on
split, poses dual
as plus. Not the most
Nagasaki
experience, though
red pivots.

stick
handle

nettle   cudgel

in the mud
asking price

Descending out-of-door
attributes. Small migrates
toward touchy-feely,
venting moments reach.
Erase amasses rush. Outdoor
journeys high, and high,
like inample, sheers
floatality.
Down the waft
nominates unique
as much as path
speaks elongation.

toll for thee
squad

wheels within
vector

spoils of

Lapsarians of the antipyre
porous with possession. Alpine
only as remains. Cursives
not defined as blue
for love nor money. In-
inversion. I or else
their happy families
who fuss with grey.

flotsam and
of straw

one's
last gasp

You who heave at blind, who
press a phrase from truss.
Once in lake and twice afloat:
were you seldom tone?
Beyond maintains
excuse, assumes a manual
for ampersands
who have no tag. Bound
from view, at home
persists as pull.

less
minus delete

deep six
picket

backspace
scratch

Neither food nor arm nor
iron-shod impending. Whatever
was pledged remains at hand, whatever
impedes resembles. Do you remember
the air over capital gain? Enormous
they purchased the grist
and substitutes for mills.

flowing with milk

it never rains
but

However has another want
across the scab who sends.
Whose next avoids. We hurdle
hues not fallen—what we shunt
from wove, they exhaust
from stammer. Falter
kneading mute.

fill it up

piece of

Aggressive Leisure

Savours filter, a
lunge at termination—

limos offer public tags.
I'm glad in fact of re-runs

culled from arson,
evidence, indications &

an almost insufficient
alias: shared passion

for indoor votes, importance
in the long run—

in the no-fly zone—
re-runs

of a million deeply
genuine absentees

asleep in strata, whose
slurs evade

the volumetric
higher cost—

a fact avoided
"just in case"

but only slip-shod
equals soft &

witness gleans
tonnage, refracts

the proudly veined, a nest-egg
or some warranty

prevention, sunburst
amplitude

a kind of suit
or broken heart—

a Yeti?
Papers tell us

nearly one
in every three alive

passes full of newsy bounce—
lumber never answered, it

fell in heaps
forgotten wars &

modes of buck
all set for go-ahead, set

for bush-league
space ports, clingy

on the outer
colonies

Stabled

Stabled during and menagerie
of recourse on a slope, terraced
swallow at the foot, in the middle
by the granite. Hold in the north
of fall below an eldest toll, where
only shores remark.

Fence fills exactly, forcing
oneself out again, a plausible quick
yet articled doze shrugs tones

gains quick as fact. Figment
happens, empties surge, yields
a note and fuses truly

from fatigue. Width in tick's advantage
trails each hometown reservoir of wannabe
medieval in my wallet. They squad Germanic

huts. Fen hooves a map
for trees, tiled by a Bible. When sprawl
hedged, kiln sprung gentle.

The largest of
            (extending over)
was once
            (which is)
and which were
            (was then)
deer were
            (the park was)
in about
            (they were)
was.

Were I whom to my cost come fuming with packs of
cross-sections, rounded into shells of so cruel a virtue
of necessity . . . were I then not in aerial oscillation, a
circuit swelled with slender glitters in brocade to hang
flaxen in this pack: it was growing dark. We stood
below the high-tension conductors, casting a
glance at the strangely inspiring curves of their
slender cables . . . those trifles come as treasures
from the heart that thinks of no remove. Perhaps, on such a
summer day as you lie in the shadow of a bush, it may
happen that your eyes are captivated by the wandering
floods, spellbound by their ripe, whom none, whom baskets—

salutes my paradise with borrowed

innocence, but . . . . in the wrong . . . . . . won't go

beyond enough . . . . . . no more

above and . . . . while . . . . . . false impression

hangs on . . . . . . boulevards, learn

. . . . . . fussy roundabouts

A Vast Tract Of Unenclosed Wild
launched by
A Hollow Stretch Of Whitish Cloud
lumped together with
This Pallid Screen
to indulge in
The Darkest Vegetation
consigned to
An Instalment Of Night
scrutinizing
An Astronomical Hour
supposed to escape
The Distant Rims Of The World And Of The Firmament
stemming from
Young Blood
plunged at
The White Gleam Of Falling Water
prompting
Mere Complexion
to underwrite
The Unusual Loiterers
by rejecting
Shaking And Dread
surviving
One Dark Mistiness
now emerging to suggest
The Gloom Of The Trees
considerably improves
The Spurs Of The Hills
invested in
The Great Masses Of Greyness
which welcome
A Weird And Solemn Effect
by sitting on
Thoughts And Grim Fancies

Slums the Norman half amen: password dun
was never lewd to bone though restaurants
were humidor and cling in happenstance
sent pelting to the restless clientele.
They safely stay some butch of Hastings
throng perchance to hood

Plugs expensive outskirts flaxen
intersects revere and swift of fair
in stucco aisle to do: blitz
abandoned, fringe fated. Haunts
the park as diva thesis carries
trickling to embankment
rung for rendezvous. Sparkling eyes
plus lasting enterprise including
painted gloves for hire

A Black Tooth in Front

a spherical distribution of matter
a vision of trees, abdomen presses
about ten billion billion times
the mass of a proton, above
the sandy desert, above the trees, above
the waves the sun, absolute zero
accelerated motion, accents of our native
tongue, accustomed road, aching
eye, aching like a bridge, across
the idle brain, act on the thumb
actions of the eye muscles, additional
spatial dimensions, admiring eye
adventurer's hair, advocated
"designer" black holes, after a few
deep breaths you inhale, after
resting the palms, after securing
the head position, after sunset
or by moonlight skies, after the bang
against a lady's ear, air
is still through many a cloud, albatross's
blood, alders near the river
alimentary canal, all ear
but never long without the heart
all her twinkling stars, all the vertebrae
benefit from the stretch, almost might
supply desert, alone on a wide
wide sea, along its lateral
side, along its medial side
along the desert, altered eye
of conquest, amber honey from the mountain
among the ancient trees, among
the dead man's hair, among
the scattered stars, among the stars
amplitude of waves an alpine spire
an exhalation, an infant's

finger touched my breast, an old
        man's hair, an opening called
the pupil, an unknown tongue
        ancient tongue, and placing your right
heel at the root of your left thigh
        another sun, antimatter
versus matter, antiparticles
        antistrings, any chosen temperature
any foot unworn, any
        other species, arched roof
of the mouth, arches of the foot, architecture
        of the heart, arctic sea, area
of the black hole's horizon, arena
        within which the events of the universe
take place, arise from neighboring
        bony structures, around his golden
hair, around my heart, as if
        a human hand were there, as the spine
and chest are fully extended
        as the sun declines, as the sun
retired, as will fill up the space between
        as you exhale, ascending roar
of desert floods, ass without an ear
        at his feet with steadfast upward eye
at his mouth inbreathe, at the foot
        of that same rock, at whose
house, atoms, attentive ear
        auditory pathway, auditory tube
autumn grave, awakened earth and
        sky, azure field, azure
fields of snow, balance your whole
        body except your right leg, bare
bleak mountain speckled thin
        with sheep, bare branch of a half-
uprooted tree, bare nerve

fibres, basketlike arrangement of nerve
fibres, bathed in human blood
       bear the body weight on the wrists
and hands, beauteous terrors of the
       earth, becalmed on sultry seas
become tubular and form hair follicles
       becomes continuous with the skin, before
the sun was up, behind the teeth
       beloved by the sun, below the
esophagus (or gullet), bend and widen your
       elbows, bend your right knee
and sit on your right foot bending
       your arms at the elbows, bending your trunk
forward and resting your chest on your right
       thigh, beneath a goodly old
oak tree, beneath a sun
       that wakes, beneath so beautiful a sun
beneath the crags, beneath the eyeball
       beneath the flowery thorn, beneath
the moon, beneath the sun, beneath trees
       bent flower, beside the lake
best blood, best fingers
       better my tongue were mute, better
sun from that long wintry night
       between 5 and 6 million
red cells in each cubic
       millimeter, between my breast-
plate and my skin, between the pelvic
       rim and the floating ribs, between
the trees beyond the sun, beyond
       the tomb, bicuspid valve, bind
the earth and sky together, bird and
       flower and stone, black blood
rolled adown, black cloud
       black cloud that hangs and threatens

black hair and vivid eye and
          meager cheek, black hole
in the heavens, black-hole entropy
          blade of the scapula, blazing sun and
beating shower, blazoned on a cloud
          bleak rock, blessed shadow
of this earth, blood comes there
          blood cries out for blood
blood dances freely, blood
          hounds, blood in the heart chambers
blood is not a simple liquid
          blood must stream, blood
of all the house, blood of an unhappy
          man, blood sometimes clots
within a vessel, blood with cold
          blood within her froze, bloody
sun at noon, bloody war
          blow through my ear, blue
ethereal field, blue flower
          blue sky above, blue sky to
many a prisoner's eyes, bluntly
          pointed portion, blush for the crime
in blood, body bears the strain
          and becomes more elastic, body's
weight is carried to this arch, boiling
          sea, bones of the foot, bones
serve as levers, borders of the lake
          borne on the head alone, bosom
of a placid lake, both muscles flex
          the wrist, both palms supported
from the earth, both the lumbar and the
          dorsal regions of the spine benefit
bottom of my heart, bounteous hand
          bower where first she owned
boy of flesh and blood, braided

hair, brain grew hot, brain is
one large mass, brain
        like lightening, brain so wild, brain
through shadows stretch, brain turns
        wild, branch of the eight cranial
nerves, branches of the leafless trees
        branchless ash, brave tongue
breathing will be very fast and laboured
        breathless field of light, breezy
air, the sun, the sky, bright
        flower of hope, bright on a rock
the moonbeam played, bright star
        bright stars of ice, brighter
cloud, bristling of the fur or ruffling of the
        feathers, broad flat annular
band of smooth muscle, broadening
        sun, brook and bridge and grey
stone cottages, broom in flower
        brother's blood, brown skeletons
of leaves, budding trees, built
        a bridge, buried among trees
burning soil, burns like one
        dilated sun, burnt down
to a finger-joint, burrow in the earth
        bursting sun, busy human
heart aweary, but in the brain
        by keeping it parallel to the floor
by lakes and sandy shores, by nature's
        hand prepared, by rivulet or spring
or wet roadside, by the frost foreclosed
        by the moonlight river side, by the side of a
river both deep and great, caged
        within the flower, calm glossy
lake, canopy of firs, cardiac
        muscle resembles skeletal muscle

cardiac orifice, careless as a flower
        carries capillaries and nerves to the hair
carries waste materials away
        carry the sound waves to the tympanic
membrane, cast the sad eye to
        earth, catch the right big
toe by bending the right knee
        cavern's mouth, cells produced
by red bone marrow, cells
        with many slender extensions, central
artery of the retina, cerebellum
        cerebrum, channel of rock stone
the ruinous river, chest on the floor
        and relax, chilled each tongue to
silence, chilled heart, church-yard
        with sear elm-leaves strewed
circumscribed elevation on a bone, city
        gates will fly open, city
pomp, city silent as the moon
        city with banners all streaming, city-
crowds must push, class of black
        holes, cleft the mountain's front
cling with poisonous tooth, close
        by this river, in this silent shade, clothe you
with rainbows, cloud over mid-day's
        flaming eye, cloudless skies
cloudless, starless lake of blue
        clouds rise thick with heavy lowering
clouds that crest the mountain's brow
        clouds that gather round the setting
sun, clouds the misty brain
        clusters of galaxies, clutched my hair up
coal black hair, coast
        the silent lake, cold blast of the
tree, cold grave, cold

season, come down without bending the legs
common earth, common flexor
	tendon, common sun, companion
of the morning star at dawn, composition
	of the brain, comprises an unevenly shaped
shell of cartilage and skin, configuration
	that a string can use, connecting one
region of the universe to another, consisting
	of three quarks, consists of skin
conspicuous flower, construction of the valves
	contact with the pupil's circular margin
contains only cone cells, contains the
	receptors of hearing, continuous
as the stars, continuous
	protoplasmic mass, cooling
stream, core of an atom, core
	of my heart, corneal margin, corner
house, corresponding ventricle
	cots, and hamlets, and faint city-
spire, could my heart's blood
	give, countenance of the horizontal sun
covers but not hides the sky, cranial
	cavity, cranial nerves arise
creature of the earth, creep on tiptoe
	round this house, cross section
of hair, crowded firs, crowded
	over my brain, crowned wither
dewy star, cultured field
	curled-up dimensions, curses
on my tongue, curvature of spacetime
	dancing rocks, dark eyes and
glossy locks, dark frowns
	the rock, dark green adder's
tongue, dashed him to the earth
	dashed to earth, day and nights,

summer and spring, dead calm
        lake, death's dark house
deep and even breathing, deep in the
        tyrant's heart, deep is the sky
and black, deep radiance of the setting
        sun, deep red of the mucous membranes, deep
the river was and crusted
        deep-trod foot marks
deflects the hand laterally, delicate
        circular membranous band, delicate
fingers on the snow, delight in the things
        of earth, water, and skies, depressions and
elevations of bone, desert air
        perfumes, desert cell, desert
lands reflect our blaze, desert
        pines ascend, desert sands
rise up, desert shouts
        desert wilderness, desert's heart
desolate in heart, desperate hand
        dewdamps of the charnel house
diameter of the pupils, did constant
        meditation dry my blood?
dimension with which we are already
        familiar, dirge and faltering tongue
disappointment's wintry desert
        fling, disheveled hair all madly
disinherited of earth, distance
        between successive peaks or troughs
of a wave, distracted brain, dizzy
        in a brain, dizzy rocks, do not hold
the breath, dome of the skull, done
        through the nose, doubling of the known
elementary particle series
        down beneath the trees, down that
sunless river, down the street

down the wind from lake or stream
down to a sunless sea, dragged
        from their hovels, dreams on the banks
and to the river talks, drear desolate
        whiteness of his fields, dreary sea
flows drifting on a field of ice
        driven from their house and home, drop
of blood, drops of that poor infant's
        blood, drops on the cheek of one
he lifts from earth, drunk with human
        blood, ducts open by minute
orifices, due to the lateral
        twist of the trunk, due to the stretch
of the neck, due to the tension of the spine
        during exhalation, dusky
corners of this house, dusky hair
        dwellings among trees, dwells a cloud
before my heavy eyes, dwindled
        woods and meadows, dying heart
dying sovereign's ear, each finger
        contains three phalanges, each flower
that binds the breathing locks of spring
        each hair of his head was alive, each hand
each heart its wonted pulse forgets
        each heavy eyelid, each inhalation
each sinew powerless, each tongue
        eager eye, eager tongue
eagles, play-mates of the mountain's
        blast, ear converses with the heart
ear unstunned, ears so raw and
        red, ears throb hot
earth and stars composed
        a universal heaven, earth
and water on the stumps of trees, earth
        groaning from beneath them, earth has

taken the infection, earth heaved
          under them with such a groan, earth
helped him with the cry of blood, earth in a
          dizzy motion, earth in fast thick pants
was breathing, earth's rosy star
          and of the dawn, earth's groaning
earthly task to watch the skies
          earthward bend an ear, ease
her own full heart, eased a
          fretted brain, echoes ominous
over the streets, edges of the cusps
          fit closely together, egg-
shaped protective encasement for the brain
          electromagnetic field, eleven
spacetime dimensions, elliptical
          gap separating the open lids
elm-shadowed fields, encephalon
          ends in a broad tendon, energy carried
by an electromagnetic wave, energy
          carried by waves or particles, energy
embodied by a string wound around a
          circular dimension of space, entangled
in her hair, entirely beneath consciousness
          and quite involuntarily, error
shedding human blood, even but
          fast breathing, evening star
every field and bank and brae
          every foot might fall
every human heart, every
          pebbly stone, every tongue
evolution of a physical
          system from one phase to another
exerts a fine adjustment to the tone
          of the muscles, exerts a squeezing action
on the blood, exhale, exhale again

exhaling and lowering both hips
to the floor, expand to make
your breathing long and gentle,
expanse of the universe, expansion
of the heavens, exposing those ears
to the wind and the rain extend
the kind hand, extended dimension
external acoustic meatus, eye is
like the star, eye reverted views
that cloudless day, eye shall dart through
infinite expanse, eye sublime
eye that marks the gliding creature
eye that prowled around, eye that
rolled around, eyeballs burnt
eye-balls start, eyebrows
arch above the eyesockets
eye-brows wildly haired and low
eyelash on my cheek, eyes grow dim
eyes streamed with tears, face down
with the hands stretched back, face
of war, faculties of eye and ear
faint splash, fainting ear
fair light of dawn, fair
river, fair the high grove
the sea, the sun, the stars, fair trees
and gorgeous flowers, fairest face
on earth, fairest star, fall
dizzy rocks, familiar space
around us   has three dimensions
familiar spacetime   has four
fancy's eye, fancy's heat
redounding in the brain, fanged with
frost, far-off sun
fast by a grove of fir, fast-
rooted trees, fatty material

favoured eye, favoured fields
          fearful, fearful tree, feeble
heart, fellow creature's blood
          felt in the blood and felt
along the heart, felt the sea-breeze
          lift their youthful locks, fermion
ferns still waving in the river breeze
          fertile fields, fertile fields
laid waste, fervent tongue
          fever round the languid heart
few drops of blood, fibrous
          coat of the eyeball, fibrous connective
tissue, fibular shaft, fickle star
          field of death, field or forest
fields and woods, fields, forests,
          ancient mountains, ocean, sky
fierce waves, fiercer hands
          find access to a monarch's ear
find the sun itself too hot
          fine skin, fine tongue
finely-frenzied eye, finger and
          thumb bones, finger of mortality
finger shield of industry, fingers as
          busy as bees in a hive, fingers
interwoven both hands, fir
          groves evermore, firmest
heart, first silver star
          first star through fleecy cloudlet
peeping, first the right foot
          on the root of the left thigh, first
three minutes after the big bang
          first tooth erupts between the sixth
and ninth month, fitted to the arched
          roof of the skull, fixed eye
fixed his eye, fixed on my heart

fixed the deadly tooth, flashes
shoot from heart to brain, flashes the
            golden coloured flower fleeced with
moss, fleshless man, fleshy
            ear, fleshy masses on each side
of the palm, fleshy world
            flex your right elbow, flexible
eye-brows, flexor tendon
            flexors of the fingers
flings to earth her tinsel-glittering
            vest, floated gently by eddy
currents, floated it down on the course
            of the river, floor of the mouth, flow
of time slows down, flower and
            bud together fell, flower
and tree, flower of all that springs
            from gentle blood, flower of hope
flower that must perish, flung
            the blood into my head, flung up
momently the sacred river flying
            fingers fleet, fold of the mucous
membrane running, fold the hands
            in front of the chest and balance, foliage
of those fairy trees, fond spirit
            that blindly works in the blood, fontanelles
food beneath a tree, foodfull
            ear, foot advanced and anxious
heart, foot should print
            earth's common grass, foot
was heard above, footless and wild
            like birds, footplate of the stapes, footstep
of some messenger, footsteps on the
            accustomed lawn, for many days
my brain, for such a brain to hold
            for us the listening heart shall gain

force transmitted to the oval
        window, force-free motion
forepart of the heel bone, forest
        and field and hill and dale appear
forgetful hand, form of flesh and
        blood, formed by the palate, fortunate
star, found in the nucleus of an atom
        foundations and the building, four
permanent teeth, the first molars, fragrant
        bower, fragrant with flowering trees
freeze the blood, frenzy stricken
        brain, fresh and alert in the mind
friend in the ear of friend, friend
        of the moon, o earth from a mother's tongue
from among the trees, from field to rock
        from her hand, from her own mouth
from his heart, from mouths of men
        from my heart in tears, from my tongue
from sky to earth it slanted, from the base
        to the neck of the spine you remain erect
from the lake a zigzag path, from the sun
        and from the breezy air, from
the wind-rent cloud, front
        of the forearm, frontal lobe
frontal section of heart showing
        orientation of atria
fronting elms, frost-ring
        hand, frosty season, frothy,
writhing, tumultuous character of the
        spacetime fabric, fruit-like
perfume of the golden furze, fruits of
        toil, fundamental one-dimensional
object, fundamental structure
        of matter, ganglion, gardens
where flings the bridge its airy span

gazing at the western sky, gazing out
upon the dreary field, gentle
    hand, genuine morning star
giddiness of heart and
    brain, gladden the green earth
gladness stirs my heart, glistening
    fibrous sheet, goes straight
like an old Roman road, gold
    star on its brow, golden finger
golden hair, goodly face
    gore-drenched field, gorgeous
tomb does lie, graceful as the fir
    graspless hand, grass and green
herbs underneath the old oak tree
    grassy alter piled with fruits
grateful hand, grateful heart
    grave with tombstone, grave your foot
is half upon, grave's green
    slope, grave-clothes, graves
all in a row, graves all side
    by side, graves and bolsters are soft
and green, gray matter covers
    great city, green field
green fields and icy cliffs
    green fields below him
green mountain, variously
    up-piled, green mountain's
side, grew in clefts and bore
    a scarlet flower, grey clouds
grey-haired man of gentle
    blood, grove and field and garden
interspersed, guillotine
    in blood, guiltless blood flowed
habitual restlessness
    of foot, haggard cheek

hair colour depends on pigment
        hair dishevelled by the pleasant
sea-breeze, hair in mazy
        surge, hair of glittering grey
hair stands on end, hairs
        are coarse and curve, half a foot
in height, half hid by rocks and
        fruit trees, half-confessing
eye, half-sheltered hovel
        half-shut eye, hamstrings
on the back, hand outstretched
        hands down on the floor
hang down from the nape of the neck
        harvest field, haste but
to the grave of the beloved, haunting in her brain
        hay and corn-sheaves in one
field, he fit his tongue, he grasped
        my hand, head of the femur, head to
foot, heart a prey to inward
        woe, heart as sensitive
to joy and fear, heart at once
        and eye, heart could not sustain
heart did of a sun so sweet, heart
        forlorn, heart revolts within
heart that dallied with distress, heart
        to cheer heart with hollow joy
heart's blood, heat of brain
        heaven's bright causeway paved with
stars, hedge your tongues about
        heedful heart, held in place
as they cross the wrist, helm of cloud
        her brother's eye, her eye was busy
while her fingers flew, her face
        reflected, her hair was thick with many a
curl, her smiling mouth, heroic

          tongue, hesbane and aconite
on a mother's grave, high as the sun
          high in these alps, hilly fields and
meadows and the sea, his black matted
          hair on his shoulder is bent, his brain
will burn his stout heart split
          his ears they stun, his finger moved
his flashing eyes, his floating hair
          his tongue hangs out hissing through
my brain, hold it to my ear, hold the posture
          as long as you can, hold the tears
to the surface of the eyeball, holding this pose
          from 20 to 30 seconds, holes of his
eyes and the hole of his mouth, hollow
          eye, hollow muscular organ
hollow shafts of compact bone
          hollow trees, holy river
holy star, honeyed tongue
          honour drinks its blood, horned
moon with one bright star
          house and land, house at night
behind some sheltering stone, house
          furniture, house is doomed in fire
house nor cottage, huge broad breasted
          old oak tree, hunger's
tooth, I am of flesh and blood
          I bit my arm, I sucked the blood
I climbed the mountains height
          I could lay my finger on it
I have drank the blood since then
          I lay with brain, I looked upon
the rotting sea, I saw them turn
          to blood, I too dug
the grave, icy hand, idle
          tongue, if both hands release

if the brain be full, if the fingers
      are not loosened, if the pelvic area juts
forward, imprisoned lake
      in a dead man's ear, in a place of
tombs, in a sitting posture, in a sunny
      field, in branches and in stars, in city
garret pent, in common with the stars
      in concord with his river, in dim cave with
bladdery sea-weed strewed, in folly's
      eye, in front of the cerebellum
in heart as dull in brain, in my arms
      in the desert places of the earth, in the
human eye, in the leaves a little sun
      in the number of white cells, in the open
air each limb, in the sun at ease
      in the tonsillar sinus, in the world's eye
in this unknown flower, increases the gastric
      fire, industrious sun, inexperienced
heart, infant hand, infection may
      spread from the nose, infinite space
ingredients in string theory, inhale
      raising your head up, inland
sky, inner bony wall
      of the middle ear, innocent and grateful
heart, insensitive epidermis
      inside of the earth, interbrain
interlock the fingers and place the palms
      on the floor, into an unblest grave
into that silent sea, into
      the bones of the hand, into the bones of the
wrist, into the cavern's mouth
      into the deserts, into the west
intruding sky, isle of the river
      it caught his eye, it cools my blood
it cools my brain it raised my hair

it fanned my cheek, it seems to live
upon my eye, its companion
        vein, its head on earth recline
its path was not upon the sea
        its shaded mouth, jet black
hair in pearly braids, jutting
        rocks, keen eye, keep the
tongue passive, keep them stretched
        straight with the feet together, keeping the
back erect, keeping your head up
        keeps the earth down tight
kick the legs and stretch them straight
        kind heart, kindly star
knocked against the walls of the arteries
        knot of spiry trees, known as a
mirror pair, labours of my hand
        lake in evening light, lake in the
midst, lake or river bright
        and fair, lakes and famous hills
land of luxury, languid eye
        lank space and scytheless time
with brawny hands lap their blood
        large house, large mass of
nervous tissue, large spatial
        extent, large uppermost
part of the brain, larger blood
        vessels arise, later enclose
the hair, lateral part of the eyeball
        lateral, medial, posterior, latitude and
longitude, laughed on their shores the hoarse
        seas, lead into the sea, left
palm over left heel, legs
        apart sideways, legs together and
straight, without any jerks, length of
        hair let loose through its streets

let the kiss speak what is in my heart
            leveled to earth, liberal hand
lid margins, lies in his grave
            lies on the floor of the cranial cavity
lies to the ear and lies to every
            sense, lift my hand against
lifts up his eye from the earth, light
            breaks through clouds, light heart
light of sun and star, light to the
            sun and music to the wind, lightening-
flash athwart the brain, like a being
            on the sea, like the flower of the rock, like
the star of eve, like venom though her brain
            lily finger, lime-tree
bower, lined by mucous membrane
            lingering star forlorn, lips and
hair of hungry white, lips
            turn pale, listen to the proper
sound of the passage of air, little field
            of meadow ground, little fingers
touch, little fountains, sparkling in the sun
            little home within my heart, little lot of
stars, live in the upper sky
            lived in a hollow tomb, living
flowers that skirt the eternal frost
            locks of his white hair, lodge the
semicircular ducts, lone and
            melancholy tree, lonely
as a cloud, lonely field, lonely
            house, lonesome chapel at the mountain's
feet, long slender bone
            long, long comfortless roads
longer as the neck shoulders abdomen and
            spine become stronger, looming
on a distant horizon, loose luxuriance

of her hair, love the city's
gilded sky, love's tomb
        low voice to my particular ear
lower the feet until they touch
        the sides of the shoulders, lower the legs
behind the back, lowermost
        part of the brain, lowliness of heart
lumbar region of the spine feels the
        stretch, luminous cloud, lunar
beams, made my tongue his organ
        main road, mainly flexors, maintain
a firm grip on the toes, maintain the
        pose for as long as you can, make your back
as concave as possible, mane of daughter
        maniac's hand, many a feeling
heart, many a gorgeous flower is
        duly fed, many a shrub
and many a tree, many an endless
        endless lake, many tinted
streams and setting sun, margins of the
        lids, mark her grave, mass of a
quark or an electron, mass of the buttock
        masses of glandular tissue, master-
current of her brain, mastication
        swallowing the sense of taste and speech
maternal fingers, matrix of the nail
        matter and antimatter annihilate
one another, maximum height of a
        wave peak, may he whose eye
is over all protect you
        may well afford to mortal ear
maythorn tree, meadow's pleasant
        green, meadows hills and groves
medial part of the orbit, medulla
        oblongata, melancholy

mountain's head, mellowing sun
         melt only at the sunbeam ray
of gold, melting eye, melting in her
         eye, melts on her ear, membranous
envelope, mesh of loose connective
         tissue, messenger particle of the weak
force, microscopic constituents
         midbrain, midnight stars outshining
milk or baby teeth, minimal
         possible mass, mirth of the loosely-
flowing hair, modified horny
         layers of the epidermis, mole-
eyed, moment's space, moon that
         meets, moon was lost behind a
cloud, moonlight and stars and empty
         streets, moonlight path over flowering
weeds, moping head, more blood
         circulates there, more of soul
in his face than words on his tongue, morning
         star of my best joys, morning
sun, morsel to my mouth, most eloquent
         mouths, most resplendent hair, motion
of our human blood, motley market
         motor fibres, mouldering in the grave
mouldy vaults of the dull idiot's
         brain, mountain bee in May's
glad ear, mountain crags
         mountain foot, mountain surges
bellowing, mountain's edge, mountain's
         glitering head, mountain's head
mountain's matchless height, mouth
         cavity, mouth of yonder cavern
mouths of innocents, mouths to feed
         move both legs together, inch
by inch, move your leg down

            sideways to the floor, mucous
membrane laid on dense fibrous tissue
            mucous membrane of the middle ear
multidimensional hole, multi-
            verse, muscle exerts traction
on the bone, muscle fibers fused
            muscle of the knee joint, muscles
act reciprocally, muscles arise
            from a fibrous ring, muscles in the region
of the hip, muscles that move the eyes
            music dies upon the ear, music
lulled your infant ear, must eyes
            be all in all the tongue and ear
mutinous clouds, my anguished eye
            my anxious eye, my brain grew hot
as fire, my brain shall burn for
            hours, my brother's grave, my burial
vault, my foot the hidden margin
            roves, my heart was faint, my mountain
grave, my own flesh, my own
            road, myriads of daisies, myrtle
flower, myrtles fearless of the mild
            sea-air, mysterious earth
nail and its neighboring parts, nail
            rests on the nail bed, nameless
rivulet, narrow fibrous line of
            union, narrow streets, native
lake, naturally occurring anti-
            matter, near the navel, near the
tranquil lake, neck and shoulder
            muscles stretch fully, neither
road nor path nor foot to tread
            nerve supply to the vessels of the heart /
muscle, nervous coat or retina
            nether seas upthundering, network

of vessels, neutrino, neutron, never-
              bloomless furze, new-born
honey-dropping flower, new-
              thawed sea, whose sudden gulphs
nipping frost, no blood stains
              no earthly tongue could ever tell
no friendly hand, no hand to grasp your
              dying hand, no more her breath
can thaw their fingers cold, no one's
              ear, no pressure should be felt
inside the ear, noble house
              non-gravitational forces, noonday
sun, nor shout nor whistle strikes
              his ear, nor will he turn
his ear aside, normal curvatures
              of the spinal column, not the value
of a hair, now a tranquil sea
              now heavy eye, nuclei
in the midbrain, nutrient artery
              o blood hounds, o
star benign, oak that in summer
              was pleasant to hear, oars into the silent
lake, objects can pass through barriers
              that should be impenetrable, oblique
muscles run diagonally, occupied by bone
              cells, occupied by the tongue, odd's my
fingers of ancient mountain, and beneath
              the clouds of caves and trees, of dewy
glitter gems each plant and tree
              of house and field, of one blood
our veins are filled, of royal eastern
              blood, old broad-trodden
road, old mossy bridge
              old ocean claps his hands
on a lonesome road, on a

mountain's highest ridge, on earth's
uneasy scene, on every tongue
          on her fingers, on his smiling face
on its sunny bank the primrose, on lake or
          wild savannah, on summer fields
on that sea-cliff's verge, on the brain
          and to the eye, on the forearms and hands
on the hot stones and in the glaring sun
          on the lake the silver luster sleeps
on the mountain's head, on the outer side
          of the ankle, on winding lakes and rivers
wide, one foot in the grave
          one human face, one
in each eyelid, one star
          reflected near its marge, one thousand
kilowatt hours, one visible space
          one whose brain, only your abdomen
bears the weight of your body on the floor
          open field, open heart
and tongue, open mouth, open
          string, opened and closed passively
by blood currents, optic axis
          optic nerves enter the orbit
or annual flower, or ear or sight
          organ connected by its root, organ of
hearing, organs of his bodily eye
          organs press against the floor
orphan's tongue, ossicles of the middle
          ear, our best blood, our common
parent's grave, our house-top
          our life's star, our sea-bird
sang, our universe is but one of
          an enormous number of separate and
distinct universes, out among the trees
          out of the carver's brain, out of the

sea came he, outer surface
of a ball, over him her golden
hair, over his friend's grave
over nerve and blood, over the
earth, over the mountain-wastes
over the piled earth, overall
motion of a string, overset the brain
or break the heart, pale moon-shaped
area at the proximal end of the body
panting tongue of thirsty skies
part of the ear consists of a spiral
passage, particle acted upon by a
strong force, parts of the brain
concerned with smell, passed the flagging
sea-gale weak, past-
future axis, peace be
on his tongue, peace on earth
pelican and ostrich of the desert, pencil
in hand and book upon the knee
penitential desert, pensive
ear, perilous seas, phalanges
photons are the quanta of the
electromagnetic
field, piercing deep the lake
pigment cells, pigment of the red
cells, pitying eye, place
his hand beside his ear, place of
tombs, place your left palm
on your hip, place your right palm
about a foot away from your right
foot, place your right palm
over your right heel, plasma
is a sticky fluid, plasma proteins
perform important functions, plays
at will the virgin heart, pleasant

with a heart at ease, plunge into the
gentle river, poesy a tongue
pons, pop out between
each finger, populous village
positively charged particle
posterior border of the soft
palate, posterior part of the foot
posterior poles of the eye, precipitous
black jagged rocks, presenting
many radial ridges, preserves his
native city, press the heels to the
floor, press the upper part of the
feet with the wrists, pressed beneath
her hair, pressed closely palm
to palm and to his mouth, pressure of the
abdomen against the floor, pricking
of the blood, pride of the city, pride
that people's space, printing desert
sands, prison house, private
ear, produce pure energy
promising higher-dimensional
supergravity, prospect-bounding
sea, proteins, fats, and fatty
substances in a watery medium, prove
by your ears, what we guessed from
your tongue, pull the trunk, pulley of fibro-
cartiledge, pulmonary and
aortic valves, puny cataract
falls on the lake, purer robes
than those of flesh and blood, purge
the earth, purpled the mountain's
broad and level top, quadriceps
on the front, quanta, queen of the stars,
quickening in the heart, rack
her gentle heart, radiating fibers

rain pours down from one black
        cloud, raise your head from the floor
raise your trunk, pulling your body
        up, raised earth and gales of
evening, raising your hips up too
        from the floor, rapid river flowing
without noise, raptured eye, read
        with gentle heart, ready ear
to lend, reason has an eye, recent
        tomb, receptor mechanism
in the inner ear, receptors
        for pain, red cells differ
from all other cells, red lightnings
        from the over rushing cloud
red-cell is short lived, reduce
        the movements of the stapes, redundant
hair, reeking fields reflected from
        the mountain's side, reflection's hand
region of the pharynx above the soft
        palate, release your inner ears
repeat the pose on the left side
        replace red cells in the blood
represented in the temporal
        lobe, rest for awhile, rest
the crown of the head on the feet, rest the
        outstretched right leg on the floor
rest your legs over your head
        resting your hands on them, rests
upon the floor of the skull, rib
        cage should expand both forwards
and sideways, ribbed sea-sand, rich
        cloud, rich supply of blood
right across the lake, rigid
        stems of heath   and bitten furze
ring of earth, rippling stream or

cloud reflecting lake, rise like a
cloud of incense from the earth, rising
           sun, river did glide, with wind
and tide, river flow with ampler
           range, river flows through the vale
river glides the woods, river
           murmuring near, river now with
bushy rocks, river steep and
           wide, road conducted me through
countries, road of duty, road
           the human being travels, rock
at night, rock fruit or flower
           rock hewn steps, rocks and
quivering trees, rod with a swelling
           at each end, roll
upon my grave, rolled down the river
           roof of the orbit, rose slowly
through their mouths, rotate the right
           elbow and shoulder, rotationally
symmetrical, round which
           the screaming seagulls soar
rounded bony prominence, roused
           your blood, rude rock, rugged
northern mouths would strain, rushed
           on earth, sable hair, sacred
river ran, sad theme
           for every tongue, saliva acts
salutes the sun his veiling clouds
           sandy desert fountains, sank him to the
tomb, sank to earth in vernal
           showers, saw the sun-awakened
sky, scant white hairs
           with foretop bald, scanty brain
scarce bedimmed the star that shone
           scarcely conscious fingers scarred

by the blood, scooped earth
        scorn that crazed his brain, scuds
the cloud before the dale, sea
        meantime his billows darkest rolled
sea of blood bestrewed with wrecks
        sea's faint murmur, sea-
born breezes, sea-born
        isle, sea-cave beneath the
breezy headland, sea-green
        river, searching eye, seas of
pain seem waving through each limb
        secret as the grave, secretion of saliva
seek the city's busier scene
        seen toward the nasal side
segment of the spinal chord
        seized on the ear, self-same
grave, semilunar valves
        sensations of the skin, sent out
like fingers, separated from the
        upper surface of the diaphragm, separates it
from the middle ear, set not
        this tongue upon me, sets into a red
jelly-like mass, seven
        orbital muscles, several strata of
nerve cells, shade the eyes
        from glaring light, shadow casting
race of trees, shadow of a star
        shadow—earth's broad shade
shafts of the bones of the leg shall skin
        the wounds, shall this town become
a field of slaughter? shallow lake
        shapes that cannot be deformed into one
another, sheath within which a tendon
        glides, shed the innocent blood
sheds the setting sun a purple

gleam, sheds the sinking sun
a deeper gleam, sheep's skin
            should gain, shelter of its trees
sheltering trees, shepherd's foot
            shift your weight to the left side
shirt and skin, shirt of hair
            shooting star on high, shot
me through earth, sea and air
            shoulder blades stretch, shouting
field, showing that the universe
            is not fully left-right
symmetric, sick heart hunger
            scarcely sung, sickening heart
side of the face including the temple
            side of the tongue, sightless Milton
with his hair, silence for the pleasure of the ear
            silence of a city, silence of the cloudless
sky, silence of the sea, silent as though
            they watched the sleeping earth, silent
from the upward eye, silent mountain
            lone and bare, silent sea
of pines, silent sky, silent
            sun, sing the spring to meet
the warmer sun, singing above
            on the mountain ash, sink to the grave
sits on my grave and gazes at the moon
            situated in the dermis, situated
obliquely in the thoracic cavity, skeleton
            arms that from the mountain's trunk,
skeleton of the head and trunk, sketched
            on a strip of pinky-silver skin
skin contains five types of
            receptor, skin was as white as leprosy
skin was the same as steel, skinny
            hand, skirting trees, sky

and all its forms, sky earth river
          lake and sea, sky my fretted
dome shall be, sky to earth is
          slanted, sky was dull and dark
that night, sky-pointing peak
          sleeping on the mountain's breast, sloping
down the sky, slow foot
          slumbering in the brain, slumbering
on some mountain's head, small cells
          and a dense network of fibres, smallest
bundle of the weak force field
          smallest physical units
smooth muscle fibers of the iris
          smooth river deep and clear
smooth transparent skin, snail-
          like house not built with hands
snake's small eye, snow-
          white hairs, snug little farm
the earth, snug, in a full friz of
          hair, so many tears in our eye corners
so that your right heel is under
          your right buttock, so-called external
black holes, soft affection's ear
          soft as breeze that curls the summer
clouds, soft membrane parts
          soldier's tomb, solid phase
liquid phase, gas phase
          solitary through the desert, some
commanding star, some daffodils
          some mountain blast, some tall tree that
spreads its branches wide, some widow's
          grave, sons of blood, soon
his path the sun soothes my ear
          sorrows of her favourite flower, sound
sense in his brains, sounding trees

sounds made by the beating heart, sounds
to my ear—spacetime foam, spangled
skies, sparkling eye, sparkling
frost, speaks no longer in my heart
spindle-shaped cells, spiral
membranous tube, spires whose silent
finger points to heaven, splendour in the
grass, split apart into two
strings, split upon a rock
spongy bone, spongy substance at the
ends, spot the sunny fields
spread into a grassy lake, sprout
forth from each head like the ears, square
tomb, squeezed through small vessels
staff in hand, stain its craggy
sides with human blood, stains of
blood, standing affects our bearing
and carriage, stands in the sun, star of
aspect heavenly bright, star
of Bethlehem, star of eve
star sheds a mellowed ray
star that led the dawn, star-
dogged moon, starless cloudless
lake of blue, stars were shaped
startled ear, states of oscillation
of a physical system, steaming brother's
blood, steaming lake, steep
mountain's loftiest stage, steep
rocks and river banks, stellar
evolution, sterile brain, sternness
of the brain, stiff finger, still
building higher, and still building
still murmur of the distant sea
still radiates from the heart
still to earth, still to sojourn

on the earth, stilly murmur of the far-off
        sea, stinking henbane and dusky
flowers, stole on his ear a voice
        stone tomb, stony eyeballs
stopped nostril and glove-guarded
        hand, storm which earth's deep
entrails hide, stormy sea
        stout bands, whorls, and circles
which surround the cavities, straggling locks
        his thin grey hair, straight
in front level with the shoulder, stream of
        blood, stream so brightly flowing
stream that flows out of the lake
        stretch the legs straight again
stretched on the rock, stretching up
        string mode, string winds
around a circular spatial dimension
        strode over the reeking streets, strong as a
mountain river, strong feelings
        to his heart, strong foot, strong
ribbon like bands or cords, strong
        winds the trees annoy, strongest of the
four fundamental forces, stupendous
        mountain, such impetuous blood
sudden breeze, suffered on each finger-
        joint, sullen star, summer
noon, summer shower, summer
        torrent's gentle dash, summer's
brightest scarlet flower, summit and
        keystone of this arch, sun above
the mountain's head, sun awakened
        sky, sun broke out
in power, sun first dawned
        upon the streams, sun goes
down, sun in heaven, sun is in his

harbour, sun of bliss, sun of
truth, sunken eye, sunless
        pillars deep in earth, sunny
mist, supergravity
        supersensory ligament
of the lens, superstrings, super-
        symetric standard model, surface of a
four-dimensional ball, suspect the
        darksome fickle heart, suspension of
cells in a fluid, swampy field
        of battle, sweep the ear with lowly
wing, sweet flower, sweet
        fragrance that the wild flower yields
sweet star, sweet to Fancy's
        ear the warbled song, sweet
tree of hope, sweeter meadow
        sweetly shone the evening sun
swelling of her heart, swift over my brain
        swing your right hand behind your
waist, tachyon, take a deep inhalation
        take a few breaths, take another
deep inhalation, take the pressure of the
        body on the neck, tall tomb, talus
tangled in her hair, tarsal glands
        tawny skin, teach our feeble
tongues, tears of love shall wet
        his tomb, teased the brain, ten thousand
stars beneath, tendons in the neighborhood
        of joints, tendons of the palm of the hand
tension in the eyeballs, that last good
        gift, a grave, that silver thread
the river, the astounded ear its dull
        undying roar, the beatifying
effect of haemoglobin, the brook's
        margin, the deepest dell

the mountain's breast displays, the eye
        has three coats, the eye reposes, the eye
that greets, the foot of horse the voice
        of man, the general ear, the general
heart of human kind, the good man's
        living ear, the image of a poet's
heart, the lake below, the lantern in her
        hand, the last drop of our blood, the
meanest flower that blows, the mine's
        mouth, the moonlight desert and the moonlight
sea, the pastoral river will forgive
        the soldier's trumpet-wearied
ear, the state's parental ear
        the sun at morning and the stars at night
the tall sun, the tempting sun
        the tented field, the very hardest
heart on earth, the very sun that
        brightens, the whole wide lake in
deep repose, the wished-for sun
        their upright hair, their yellow hair
then exhale and bend your right knee
        there is no more remarkable substance
in nature than hemoglobin, there never
        foot had been, there stands the flowering
maythorn tree, there was a time
        when earth, and sea, and skies, these few
meager vales, these lapper's-up
        of blood, these tears and my poor idle
tongue, they thirst for my blood, thigh
        on the opposite hand, thimbled finger
thin and weak and blends with the fascia
        this aged tree, this clouded sun
slopes westward, this glade of water and this
        one green field, this hand
should make his life-blood flow

this mass is called a clot, this piled
earth, this protecting hand, this scene of
        earthly toil, thorns in your footpath
though the tibia, threads and hairs of
        light, three semicircular
canals, through his brain, through my brain
        through sun and rain, through the high tree
branching wide, through the streaming streets
        through wood or open field, throughout
the streets, throughout the strenuous
        movements, the mind remains passive and
still, thrown back by that same earthquake, thumb
        has only two, thunder from a midnight
cloud, tied by strong ligaments
        tight seals which prevent blood from
leaking backward, tighten your legs by
        drawing up your kneecaps, till your right
thigh is parallel to the floor, time and weary
        space, timourous and tender flower
tissues of all parts of the body
        to his heart he held her hand, to hoof and
finger mailed, to start with there will be
        perspiration and trembling, to the clouds
and to the stars, to the eye of day, to the mine's
        mouth, to vibrate on his ear, toes
nearer to the head, tomb of recent
        date, tomb's dark grass
tones the abdominal region of the body
        tongue can be turned on itself, curled up
or moved from side to side, tongue
        can't stir when mouth is filled, tongue could
whisper words of might, tongue
        devoid of gall, tongue had cloven to my
mouth, tongue is able to rehearse
        tongue is concerned with several functions

tongue never soothed, tongue not used
          to falter, tongue of calumny, tongue of
envious pride, tongue of every
          child, tongue of light, tongue-
hero, tongues have learned another
          name, tongues that trafficked in the trade
of praise, topologically distinct
          torn or forced into the atria, torrent
falls on woody mountain dell, torrent
          from the mountain's brow, torus,
total darkness overspreads the skies, touch
          the shoulders with the fingers
touched then his tongue, touching my heart
          as with an infant's finger, towns and
cities thick as stars appear
          trace with searching eye the heavenly
houses, trailing plants and trees were
          intertwined, transparent and unprotected
except by the eyelids, transparent
          mucous membrane, transverse arch
travels the sky, traversed the open
          sea, tread over graves, tree
was there, tree with leaves of feeble
          stem, trees and stones and fountain
trees creaking in the wind, trees renew
          their murmur, trees that may tomorrow
fall, trees were grey with neither arms
          nor head, trees were silent as the graves
beneath, trees, herbiage, snake-
          like stream, unwrinkled lake
trembling hand, tricks her hair in
          lovely plight, true with the tongue
try to breathe normally during all
          movements, tube-like region of space
tumbled in her hair, turbulent behaviour

of a system on microscopic scales
turn his ear and eye, turn your
        hips sideways to the right, turns
around a central pillar, twig
        from every tree, twigs of a young
birch tree, twilight shades
        darken the mountain's head, twist
wild limbs above the ferny
        rock, twitched my ear, two
almond shaped masses of lymphoid
        tissue, two bright dew-drops
bosomed in a flower, two coronary
        arteries, two dimensional surface
of a doughnut, two longitudinal
        arches, two round spaces
void of snow, two thirds of the
        heart lies to the left of median
plane, two tiny muscles
        two up-quarks and one
down-quark, tympanic cavity
        tympanic membrane, type of string
with two free ends, typical
        energy of a vibrating string, ultra-
microscopic, umbrage of her hair
        unconscious hand, under a cloudless
sun, under the shady trees
        underneath a huge oak
underneath an old oak
        tree, unfelt around my mountain
grave, unfrequented roads, unhinge
        his brain, union of space and time
union of the electric and magnetic
        forces, unrusted with the villains blood
unshaped tomb, unsigned hair
        unsteady earth, until the setting

sun, until the stars of night
            until your legs and hands stretch
in opposite directions, untrodden desert
            up a great river, great as
any sea, up to sun and
            cloud, upland road, uplift
his hand, uplifted ear, upon
            a crystal river, upon a desert
thrown upon his brain, upon his
            swinging corse an eye can glance
upon the focus of the sun, upon the
            fragrant mountain's purple side
upon the moon I fixed my eye
            upon the rapid river, upon the
slimy sea, upper lateral
            incisors appear, upper lid is
more extensive, upper part of the skull
            upper surface of the tongue shows numerous
elevations, upper third of the
            cornea, upwards to the day star
valley's playful windings, variations
            in the number of white cells, vast
river stretching in the sun, venturous
            foot, verdant hills, verdure on the
lake below, vernal field
            vernal slow-worm sun
vestibule of the mouth
            vibrational pattern
viewed as the "fabric" out of which
            the universe is fashioned, vile
sea-weed, village near the lake
            voice of the desert, wafts dreams
to Slumberer's listening ear, waist
            and chest up, walked with hair
unsigned, walls of the atria, wander

    back on such unhealthful road
waning eye, wanton in the sun
        warmth at his heart, warping of spacetime
was at your ear, wash the river
        water-lilies ripple, waving
trees, wayward brain, we
        cannot bid the ear be still
we dwell among the tombs
        weak eye glimmers, weary
eye, weary fingers, weary
        world, weight falls on the abdominal
area, weight of the body, went down to the
        sea, what she had seen and suffered turned
her brain, what time the morning sun
        of hope arose, when all parts of the
sole come into contact with the ground, when
        did the boy his tongue unlock
when the body becomes more pliable
        when the sun is down, when they climb
the sky, when through the trees, when
        to the mouth relenting death, when we stand
on our feet, we need no extra effort
        where darkness seems to guard
the mouth, where human foot did never
        stray, where my poor heart
lost all, where sun and shade
        were intermixed, where the fabric of space
or spacetime suffers a devastating
        rupture, where the heaviest foot, where you
wait for two breaths, where's the photon
        which sky and ocean smote, which smote
air, earth, and sea, which soon
        must be his grave, while bending your right
leg at the heel, while grove and river notes
        would lend, while he is balancing

on his head, while the sun sinks
            down, while your arms hang from your neck
like a garland, whirl blast
            whispered nightly to his ear, white of the
eye, who in his heart had groaned, whole
            heart, whole weak wishing
heart, whole weight of the body
            whom the comets forget not
whose boyish ear, wide around the
            trees, widow's eye, wild
bees in the sunny showers of spring
            wild hand, wild her hair
save where the laurels bound, wild
            tempestuous sea, wilder hand
willowy hedge-rows, winding
            energy, winding up his mouth, wind-
swept meadow, winter's night
            with a jump spread your legs apart
sideways four to four and one
            half feet, with a light heart
with a ready ear, with ear not
            coveting the whole, with far-heard
whisper, over the sea, with heart
            unmoved, with his heart he ceased to strive
with light heart, with never a whisper
            in the sea, with our blood, with quiet
heart, with rocks and stones and trees
            with the setting sun, with your lower jaw
hanging loose within my brain
            within the lap of the earth, and in the depths
within what space, wonder of his hand
            wooded slope of the mountain, woods
and sky and mountain, words of a forgotten
            tongue, wormhole, worn sides of the
chalky road, wraps in one light

[128]

earth, heaven, and deepest hell
yawning mouth, yearning ocean
        swelled upward, yellings of famine and
blood, yellow leaves in sun
        and wind, yellow marrow, yellow
sun from steep to steep, yet envy-
        stung at heart, yet stirring blood
in freedom's cause, young face
        your diaphragm softens, your eye
would search his heart, your hand
        upon my arm, your infant heart
your mind's eye

Printed in the United Kingdom
by Lightning Source UK Ltd.
100520UKS00001B/161